GREAT
BRITISH
RAILWAYS
50 THINGS TO SEE & DO

3 5 7 9 10 8 6 4 2

First published in 2020 by September Publishing

Illustrations by Grace Helmer
Designed by Emily Sear

Printed in Poland on paper from responsibly managed, sustainable sources
by Hussar Books

ISBN 9781912836284

September Publishing
www.septemberpublishing.org

all the
STATI⊜NS

GREAT
BRITISH
RAILWAYS
50 THINGS TO SEE & DO

Vicki Pipe
with Geoff Marshall

s
epte
m
b
er

CONTENTS

INTRODUCTION

The history of the railways in Britain is very complicated. The railways didn't grow slowly. Lots of very important events happened in a very short space of time and each one had a significant impact on the other. In fact, one of the most difficult questions to answer is, what was Britain's first railway? That all depends on what you mean by the word railway.

To begin with a railway was a path created by a set of metal tracks (sound familiar so far?) on which carts or waggons were pulled, usually by horses. They carried materials from quarries or mines quickly and more reliably than humans. These railways were usually just called 'waggonways' or 'tramways', and they were only used by people working in the mines to move things about.

But then in 1798, the Lake Lock Railroad in Stanley near Wakefield opened, allowing anyone to transport goods for a price. The fact that anybody could use the line made it a public, not a private railway. It was the first of its kind in Britain and possibly the world – and it changed everything!

Once the idea of a public railway for goods was achieved, it wasn't too long before someone realised railways might be good for transporting people too. The first few attempts at public passenger railways in Britain were a mix of those that were pulled by horses, and those experimenting with something called a steam engine.

As soon as the steam engine had been perfected there was no stopping Britain's railways. Everyone got excited and lines started popping up all over the place. Different railway companies were formed and each one was desperate to be the first to reach a new town, village, or city. Some companies didn't care if someone else had gotten there before them. They simply built a brand-new route and put their station in a slightly different place. Windsor Central and Windsor & Eton Riverside stations are great examples of this.

It's because the story of the railways is so complicated that there is always lots to look out for when you're travelling by train. From unusual stations to wonderful wildlife and unbelievable bridges, this book will take you on a journey of fifty of the most fascinating things to see and do across the railways of England, Scotland, and Wales.

CHAPTER 1

WHERE IT ALL BEGAN

See Britain's Railway Firts

Let's start at the beginning with a handy timeline, and a list of places you can see today.

1798 Lake Lock Railroad, Stanley *near* Wakefield

The first public goods railway pulled by horses. Take the two-mile walk from Outwood station in Wakefield to find the blue plaque commemorating the line, which is located on the corner of Lake Lock Road and Aberford Road.

1804 The First Steam Engine, Abercynon Station

The first successful steam engine was built by Richard Trevithick. The engine pulled a wagon carrying ten tons of iron from the Pen-y-Darren ironworks to the canal at Abercynon, where it dropped off the iron and returned to the works. It was a journey of about nine miles. A plaque and information board commemorating the event can be found at Abercynon station. A replica of the engine is on display at the National Waterfront Museum in Swansea.

1807 Oystermouth Railway, Swansea

The first public passenger railway pulled by horses. You can now cycle the route of the original railway line by following the signs for the Swansea Bike Path, between Swansea and Mumbles.

1825 Stockton & Darlington Railway, Durham

The first public steam railway, which carried coal, flour, and other goods between Stockton, Darlington, Shildon, and Bishop Auckland. The railway did also carry passengers, but these trains were pulled by horses for the first few years with just one exception. On the day the railway opened, the steam engine famously known as 'Locomotion No1' pulled carriages containing over 500 people. They became the first passengers to officially travel on a steam railway!

Today a journey between Stockton, Darlington, and Shildon will follow some of the railway's original route. Stop at Darlington station to see a large display with lots more information about the history of the line. A little further up the tracks, at North Road station, you can also visit the Head of Steam museum.

1830 Liverpool & Manchester Railway

The first steam passenger and goods railway to connect two cities. The line was instantly popular with passengers, who loved being able to travel quicker and cheaper than ever before. The thirty-one mile journey took just one hour and forty-six minutes by train. It usually took three hours by horse and coach – ouch!

Today the line between Liverpool and Manchester follows exactly the same route, stopping at almost all the same stations (although the station buildings have all been rebuilt). The station at the Manchester end of the line (confusingly called Liverpool Road) is no longer in use, but it is now part of the Science and Industry Museum.

CHAPTER 2

TRAINS

Today there are twenty-eight different companies who operate trains on the mainline British railway network. The reason why there are so many is (of course) long and complicated.

To start with, when the railways were first being built each railway line was owned by a separate company with their own name. By 1921, over 120 different railway companies existed. This was way too many, and so an act of parliament known as 'The Grouping Act' was introduced. It forced the majority of companies to merge together, creating four super-railway companies known as 'The Big Four'; the Great Western Railway, the London Midland and Scottish Railway, the London and North Eastern Railway, and Southern Railway.

Things changed again in 1948 when British Rail (usually just known as BR) took control of all four railway companies on behalf of the British Government in a process known as nationalisation. British Rail lasted for almost fifty years until the 1990s when everything went back to how it was before (well almost), with separate train companies running services on different sections of the network. This process is known as privatisation.

Ride All the Train Operating Companies (TOCs)

Can you take on the ultimate railway challenge and travel on at least one train from each TOC?

Avanti West Coast . . . . ☐

C2C . . . . ☐

Caledonian Sleeper . . . . ☐

Chiltern Railways . . . . ☐

CrossCountry . . . . ☐

East Midlands Railway . . . . ☐

Gatwick Express . . . . ☐

Grand Central . . . . ☐

Great Northern . . . . ☐

Great Western Railway . . . . ☐

Greater Anglia . . . . ☐

Heathrow Express . . . . ☐

Hull Trains . . . . ☐

Island Line . . . . ☐

London North Eastern Railway (LNER) ☐

London Northwestern Railway . . . . ☐

London Overground . . . . ☐

Merseyrail . . . . ☐

Northern . . . . ☐

ScotRail . . . . ☐

South Western Railway . . . . ☐

Southeastern . . . . ☐

Southern . . . . ☐

TfL Rail . . . . ☐

Thameslink . . . . ☐

TransPennine Express . . . . ☐

Transport for Wales . . . . ☐

West Midlands Railway . . . . ☐

To help you get started, we've created some suggested routes. Each one groups together two or three different TOCs; this way you can tick off several different companies in just one or two days.

Why not try out our suggested routes first, and then have a go at creating your own for the remaining TOCs on your list?

3 **Route 1** London Overground

The trains on the London Overground carry passengers around London without going through the very centre of zone one. From Richmond in the west, to Watford in the north, Stratford in the east and Croydon in the south (as well as a lot of stations in between). A fun way to tick off the Overground is to ride a complete 'loop' around the circle that goes from Clapham Junction to Highbury and Islington. From there, change trains but continue going clockwise back to Clapham Junction via Hoxton, Surrey Quays, and Denmark Hill. For a harder challenge, try to catch one of the limited Overground services that calls at Battersea Park. It's a station in between Clapham Junction and Wandsworth Road, but it's not often shown on the London Overground map – sneaky.

Route 2 C2C and Greater Anglia

4

The majority of C2C trains start at London Fenchurch Street. With only 18 million passengers each year, it is an often overlooked London station dwarfed by its nearest neighbour Liverpool Street station (which sees nearly 67 million passengers a year). Fenchurch Street is well worth a visit, and while the main entrance is impressive, there is a secret entrance via Coopers Row that brings you out halfway down the station's platforms.

From Fenchurch Street catch a C2C train to Southend Central station. From here, walk to Southend Victoria station (just a five-to-ten-minute walk through the town) to pick up a Greater Anglia service back into London via Billericay and Shenfield.

Route 3 Chiltern, Great Western Railway, Heathrow Express, TfL Rail

5

To catch a Chiltern train, head to London Marylebone station. Trains from here are only operated by Chiltern Railways. We'd recommend the service to Oxford. At Oxford station you can jump onboard a Great Western Railway service back into London Paddington.

At Paddington make sure you have time to find the statue of Paddington Bear on Platform 1.

Rub his nose for good luck on your travels before getting a Heathrow Express train to – that's right – Heathrow. At Heathrow don't get on a plane (unless you have a flight booked); instead travel back towards the city on a TfL Rail service. TfL Rail will take you back to Paddington.

6 **Route 4** Merseyrail

Merseyrail operate trains in and around the city of Liverpool. Their bright yellow trains are designed for commuter services, thousands of people travelling in and out of the city for work every day. This means there are fewer seats than you might find on longer-distance trains like the Great Western Railway but with more spaces to stand. Similar to the London Underground, the doors on Merseyrail always open automatically as they expect people to be getting on or off at each station.

Take a ride to any destination on the Merseyrail network. You won't be disappointed! However, you must make sure to ride the 'loop' that goes clockwise underneath the main city of Liverpool and get out at James Street, one of the oldest deep-level underground stations in the world.

Route 5 ScotRail   7

ScotRail runs almost all the train services throughout Scotland. Many of their trains journey through stunning, scenic locations that only Scotland could possibly serve up.

To catch a ScotRail train, the two obvious places to start are Glasgow (Central or Queen Street stations) and Edinburgh Waverley, where services are frequent and can take you all over the country. The newest line in Scotland is the Borders Railway. It runs from Edinburgh to Tweedbank. The original line along this route closed in 1969 but was reopened in 2015. There are hopes to extend the line even further south in the future, maybe even as far as Carlisle, to link up with other mainline routes.

Geoff's Travel Tips

Travelling on the Caledonian Sleeper is quite pricey, but there is a way to ride the Sleeper without having to actually sleep on it. After the Highlander service reaches Glasgow on its way to Fort William (between 6 a.m. and 10 a.m.), you can buy a ticket as if it were a normal local train. The same is true if travelling in the opposite direction in the evening from Fort William to Glasgow (between 6 p.m. and 12 a.m.). You just travel in the seated part of the train as a regular passenger. Bingo!

Britain's Busiest Railway Hub 8

Of all the stations in Britain, there is something special about Crewe. Six major routes come together here, making it the station where the greatest number of Train Operating Companies stop. It's a brilliant place to take a ride on a few more TOCs from your list, or to spend the day seeing how many you can spot.

Avanti West Coast go in multiple different directions from Crewe: south towards London via Stafford, Rugby, and Northampton; north towards Liverpool, Blackpool, and Glasgow; east towards Manchester; or west towards Holyhead.

East Midlands Railway has just one service an hour going east to Derby, via Stoke-on-Trent.

Transport for Wales services go west to Chester and Holyhead. One of our favourites is the Crewe to Swansea train that runs along the Heart of Wales Line. The train stops at thirty-nine stations including the remote and idyllically named Sugar Loaf station, and Llanwrtyd Wells: the smallest town in Wales and home of the World Bog Snorkelling Championships.

Northern trains operate a stopping service to Liverpool Lime Street that goes via Manchester Airport.

West Midlands Railway travel to London Euston via Birmingham. These are stopping services and can take up to three and a half hours from start to finish.

CrossCountry trains are hard to catch from Crewe as there are only four a day. One heads north to Manchester, and the three others travel south to Bristol and Bournemouth.

The most difficult of all the TOCs however is the Caledonian Sleeper. It only picks up passengers at Crewe going north very late at night (around 11.45 p.m.) or going south very early in the morning (about 5.40 a.m.).

Take a Look!

If you are visiting Crewe and have some time when you're not trying to catch a train, just a few minutes' walk from the station is the Crewe Heritage Centre. Here you can explore a collection of historical railway objects, buildings, and infrastructure. Perhaps their most famous object is the APT (Advanced Passenger Train), an experimental train built in the 1970s to test new technology. The train now lives just outside the heritage centre building and can be seen from the window of any regular passenger train leaving Crewe, heading north out of the station.

How Many Train Classes Can You Ride?

9

There are over eighty different types of train on Britain's railways – that's a lot of trains! We can't list them all, but we have chosen what we think are the more unique and interesting ones to look out for on your travels.

How can you tell what class a train is?

On the front of every train there will be a six-digit number. The first three digits tell you what class of train it is. For example, if a number reads '143607' then this is the Class 143. Easy!

Parry People Mover: Class 139

These can only be seen along the branch line between Stourbridge Junction and Stourbridge Town stations. It is a small one carriage train that runs every ten minutes (every fifteen minutes on a Sunday)

'D' Train: Class 230

The Class 230s were introduced onto the British mainline by West Midlands Railways in 2019. These trains were previously used on the London Underground's District Line. They are the second slowest trains on Britain's railways with a top speed of just 60 mph.

Royal Mail: Class 325

This is a very special train, one which we have never seen ourselves. It's not a train you can ride on, but is used by Royal Mail to transport post between London, the north west of England, and Scotland.

Pendolino: Class 390

Pendolino trains have special tilting technology that allows them to travel faster than regular trains. The trains lean to the side when travelling around curves in the track. You can travel on a Pendolino from London Euston along the West Coast Mainline all the way up to Scotland.

Javelin: Class 395

This high-speed train is run by Southeastern Railway and can reach speeds of 140 mph. They are known as Javelin trains because during the 2012 London Olympic Games they ran a shuttle service for spectators to the Olympic Stadium. Each train is also named after an Olympic athlete.

CHAPTER 3

RARE SERVICES

Visiting stations that have only one or two trains that stop each day can be a big challenge and requires careful planning. You'll need a copy of the station's timetable and a map of the railways to figure out the best day and time to make your trip. Here are the details of those stations currently with the rarest services.

Take a Rare Service

Teesside Airport, County Durham

There is currently just one, that's ONE, train a week that stops at Teesside Airport. This is a Sunday service, departing from Teesside Airport during the early afternoon on its way from Hartlepool to Darlington. Unfortunately, there is nothing to see or do at the station, which is a good twenty-minute walk from the airport itself. It might be a good idea to stay on the train, or maybe have a friend pick you up?

- -

Reddish South and Denton, Greater Manchester

These stations are next to each other on the line from Stockport to Stalybridge (you could tick both of these off in one day). Each station only gets two trains a week, both on a Saturday morning. The first on a service travelling from Stalybridge to Stockport, and the second less than an hour later travelling in the opposite direction from Stockport to Stalybridge.

- -

Pilning, Gloucestershire

Pilning station has just two trains that stop on a Saturday. Both services travel in the same direction, starting at Cardiff Central and terminating at Taunton, which means it's impossible to depart and return to Pilning station on the same day … or is it?

As a way to encourage more passengers to visit Pilning, the station's local campaign group have set up four exciting railway challenges that involve leaving the station on the morning train, and returning on the stopping train in the afternoon. Visit www.pilningstation.uk/challenges to read through the details of how the challenges work and how to compete.

Polesworth, Warwickshire

Every morning except on a Sunday, a train departs from Polesworth station heading for Crewe. Any passengers who get on the train here will need to find an alternative way home. There is no returning service. We know some passengers who take a bike with them in the morning, then on their way home they get off at the closest station on the line and cycle the rest of the way home.

Did you know?

Rare services are sometimes known as Parliamentary trains. There is some debate about what this actually means. We believe it goes back 176 years to 'The Railway Regulation Act' of 1844. This law requested that every railway company in the country provide at least one return train service, from each station, every weekday for travellers to get to and from work. Because the minimum number of services enforced by Parliament was just one train in each direction, any train service that provided a limited or rare service at a station was then known as a Parliamentary Train.

CHAPTER 4

DESIGN

The way a building looks and how it is designed can change the way we feel about it. Because railway companies want people to travel on their trains, the first step is getting them to visit a station. How it is designed is therefore VERY important.

What makes a great railway designer?

You might think being a great designer for the railways is all about understanding the maths and science behind how things work. While that helps, being artistic and creative is just as important as being able to add things up.

Visit Newcastle Central station, for example, and marvel at its incredible curved iron roof built in 1850. It was designed by a local architect, John Dobson, who began his career as an artist making designs for local fabric weavers and studying watercolour painting in London. Normally the iron beams used in construction were straight, but Dobson wanted his roof to curve so he invented a set of rollers that would bend the iron into the shape he wanted. Look out for a plaque at the station that celebrates Dobson's work, which still stands 170 years later.

Visit an Award-Winning Station

Montpelier Station, Bristol

Stop at Montpelier station to see *The Fearless Four Seasons* mural. Inspired by the local community and created by local artist Silent Hobo, the artwork won 'Best Community Art Scheme' in the Community Rail Awards, 2018.

The work is 15.25 metres long and runs the entire length of the station platform. The theme of the four seasons was chosen to fit with the plants, trees, and bushes that are all around the station. Local people got involved by sharing their thoughts and feelings about what the four seasons meant to them and their ideas were then incorporated into the design.

You may notice the entire station building is also covered in a mural, designed and painted by the same artist. Until there was artwork on the walls, the station building was regularly vandalised. Miraculously, once the murals appeared there was no more vandalism. The magic of design!

London Bridge Station

This station was completely redesigned and opened in 2018 after six years of building work, and approximately 1 billion pounds was spent to make it happen. Since then, it's been given no fewer than six awards, which celebrate how incredible the station looks, as well as the positive impact the new design has had on passengers and people living in the local area.

Before 2018, London Bridge was a confusing and uncomfortable place to be. It was actually two different stations, with some trains arriving on lower-level platforms and some arriving on upper-level platforms. Now all the platforms can be reached from one main concourse, currently the largest of any railway station in the UK and bigger than the football pitch at Wembley Stadium, or so we're told. Most importantly all platforms are now completely accessible for passengers with step-free needs.

Geoff's Fun Fact

One of my favourite parts of the new station is the Western Arcade, the corridor that links the mainline station to the London Underground. As you walk through the arcade make sure you look up at the incredible arches. Some are brand new, but some once formed part of the original station viaduct when it was built in 1836.

Ordsall Chord, Manchester

It's not just stations that get the awards. Catch a train between Manchester Piccadilly and Manchester Victoria stations and along the way your train will cross the Ordsall Chord. A short section of railway track made up of bridges and viaducts over the River Irwell, which, since it opened in 2017, has received four separate awards from the Royal Institute of British Architects. Before the Chord, passengers had to find an alternative way to get across the city from one station to the other.

What makes this piece of railway so awardworthy is the way the designers creatively and effectively balanced so many different challenges. The new section of track crossed over some of the original Liverpool to Manchester Railway (the world's first intercity steam passenger railway), including the River Irwell Railway Bridge built in 1830. These sections needed to be carefully looked after, repaired, and restored. The areas around the new railway were cleared and public spaces have been built that highlight the history of the railway, as well as offering opportunities for new businesses to grow.

To build the Ordsall Chord, designers used enough concrete to fill almost six Olympic-sized swimming pools and over 4,000 tonnes of steel.

Stop by Britain's Largest Stations

12

Birmingham New Street

Birmingham New Street is the busiest station outside of London with around 140,000 passengers arriving or departing on trains every day. The entire station was redesigned in 2015 and it looks and feels like no other station in Britain.

The outside of the building is curved and wrapped in highly polished stainless steel, giving the station a very futuristic look. The steel also acts as a mirror, reflecting the surrounding buildings, and even trains as they move in and out of the platforms below. We're told that when they were building this part of the station the designers had to angle the steel sheets very carefully so that the sun didn't reflect straight off them into the eyes of the train drivers!

Inside, the roof over the main concourse is made up of seven huge domes that let in lots of natural daylight. The station has twelve platforms, which are split in half and form end A and end B (except Platform 4, which has A, B, and C sections – greedy!). Dividing the platforms up like this means trains travelling in different directions can use the same platforms, saving time and space. Knowing where the A section stops and the B section begins, however, can be a little confusing, so do make sure you're concentrating when it's your turn to catch a train. You might find yourself going in the other direction.

London Waterloo

Since the station first opened in 1848, with just six platforms, London Waterloo has grown to become the busiest station in Britain. There are now twenty-four platforms, thirty-two ticket machines (as well as a staffed ticket office), an information centre, shops and cafes, two entrances to the London Underground (linked to four separate Underground lines), and access to Waterloo East station.

As you walk around, you'll notice there are two distinct parts of the station. The main concourse and the first nineteen platforms were part of the station's redesign between 1900 and 1922. Platforms 20 to 24 were originally opened for the Eurostar in 1994.

Look up at the roof over platforms 20 to 24. It is made from glass that looks like it bends to follow the curved shape of the platforms. However, if you look more closely, you'll see that this is an illusion created by hundreds of rectangular glass panels that overlap each other at slightly different angles.

Look out for!

The Victory Arch entrance, by platforms 20 to 24, is the main way into the station and one of the most impressive doorways we've ever seen. The arch commemorates staff from the London and South Western Railways who died during the First World War. Looking up at the arch from the outside, you'll see sculptures either side of the entrance. On one side they depict war and on the other side they depict peace.

Glasgow Central

On each side of the main station building are four busy Glaswegian streets: Gordon Street, Argyle Street, Hope Street, and Union Street. They form a square and in the middle of the square, hidden by shops, cafes, restaurants, and hotels is the busiest station in Scotland (and the eleventh busiest in the whole of Britain).

What you might call the main entrance is on Gordon Street, but before you step into the building make sure you head to the corner of Hope Street and Argyle Street. This is where you'll see the incredible glass-sided bridge that carries the station platforms across the road, known locally as the 'Hielanman's Umbrella' (Highlandman's Umbrella). Take a walk under the bridge and hear the rumble of the trains as they move along the platforms above and across the River Clyde.

The first thing you'll notice as you walk onto the main station concourse is the roof. It contains 48,000 panes of glass and during the Second World War each one was painted black. This was to stop enemy planes targeting the station with bombs.

Behind the Scenes

The history at Glasgow Central goes on and on. You could write an entire book about the station and still have stories to spare. This is why, if you're twelve years old or over, you should consider booking a behind-the-scenes 'Glasgow Central Tour'. You'll be led by staff into parts of the station that are not open to the public like abandoned passages, old Victorian platforms, and vaults underneath the streets.

Spot the
Smallest
Stations

While larger stations have impressive and bold designs, smaller stations can show you unique features and reveal stories that you won't find anywhere else in the country.

Dunrobin Castle, Highlands

Stop at Dunrobin Castle to discover a privately owned station belonging to the current Countess of Sutherland (who lives in the nearby castle).

Trains only stop at Dunrobin Castle, located on the Far North Line in Scotland, in the summer between the months of April and October. You'll notice the station building looks very different from every other one along the line. As it is a private station, they didn't need to build a ticket office or any other normal station facilities. Instead they created a beautiful black and white timber building that had just two waiting areas, one for the estate staff and one for the Sutherland family. Simple.

While the main reason to stop here is to visit Dunrobin Castle itself, just a short five-minute walk from the station, do make sure you take a look inside the station building. Now a museum, it is full of artefacts telling the history of the station and the railway line in the area.

Coombe Junction Halt, Cornwall

Take a train along the Looe Valley Line and stop at the beautifully deserted Coombe Junction Halt. But don't just stand on the platform, explore the area around the station to discover two fascinating design stories.

The first takes you for a close-up look at the Moorswater Viaduct; follow the path at the end of the station platform, towards the viaduct which you will see through the trees ahead. The original viaduct, designed by Isambard Kingdom Brunel, was built in 1859, and is made of stone pillars with wooden supports on top. Less than thirty years later it was replaced by a stone and cast-iron version. Look carefully and you will see some of Brunel's original pillars just a few metres behind the new ones.

The second story takes you up the hill back to Liskeard station, following in the footsteps of nineteenth-century passengers who would have made the same climb before Coombe and Liskeard stations were connected by rail.

The gradient here is so steep it took a while before an engineering solution could be found to tackle it. In 1901, they realised a straight line wasn't the answer so instead built the track in a wide arch known as the 'horseshoe curve'. When walking here, take care on the roads as there are very few pavements and lots of bends.

If you don't fancy the walk, why not wait for the next train and experience the horseshoe curve for yourself. Notice how the driver has to reverse out of the station and wait for the guard to switch the track points so that they can start the ascent back up the hill by rail.

Find a Platform-Only Station

There are lots of stations around Britain that have no facilities other than a platform (and maybe a passenger shelter). These stations are often in the heart of the country's smallest communities, providing important transport connections. While there are no elaborate roofs or ornate gateways to marvel at, you will be wowed by the landscape and the location of these unexpected platforms.

Altnabreac, Highlands

Truly one of Britain's most remote stations right in the heart of the Highlands. If you stop here it is twelve to thirteen miles from the nearest main road (access only for small vehicles, cyclists, or walkers). The platform is long enough for a four-carriage train, has a single shelter (containing a public payphone), and an old station building that is now a privately owned house.

Gilfach Fargoed, Caerphilly

Take a train from Cardiff Central along the Rhymney Line and stop at one of the tiniest station platforms in Britain. Just under sixteen metres, it cannot even fit a whole train carriage. Anyone getting off here has to go to the front of the train, where the guard will open the door to let passengers off. There are actually two platforms here, both with shelters.

- -

Nethertown, Cumbria

Located on the Cumbrian coast, the platform at Nethertown station is right next to the beach looking out over the Irish Sea. There are two platforms, but only one in use, and just one shelter to protect you from the brisk sea winds. To get down to the beach, make your way carefully over the crossing and follow the trackside path to a tunnel underneath the railway.

- -

Sugar Loaf, Powys

You'll find Sugar Loaf, one of the best station names in Britain, along the Heart of Wales Line. The nearest town is Llanwrtyd Wells, just under three miles away. There is just one small platform at the station with a shelter, electronic information board, and a guestbook for visitors to sign their name in. Also look out for the summit sign letting you know that this part of the line is 820 feet above sea level.

Marvellous Moquettes

Good design doesn't stop at stations. Look out for all the different seating fabrics on board trains as you travel around the country. *How many different ones can you find, and which one is your favourite?*

They might look random, but all the different fabric patterns are carefully considered. They have been designed to reflect the colours of each TOC, and to make passengers feel more comfortable. As well as comfort, the designs can also be a good distraction; we've heard of families who make up ice-cream flavours based on the colours and patterns used!

Did you know?

The type of fabric used for train seats is called 'moquette'. It is a French word meaning carpet.
This is because of the way the material is woven. It is packed tightly together just like a carpet. This makes it hardwearing so that millions of bottoms can sit on it before it rips, wears out, and needs to be replaced.

CHAPTER 5

TICKETS

The First Railway Tickets

Today, there are many different ways you can buy a ticket for your railway journey. You can go online, use an app on your phone, or even buy it in person by visiting your nearest ticket office and talking to a member of staff – super old school!

When the very first public passenger railways opened it wasn't as easy. Tickets were handwritten, which as you can imagine could take a while, and only noted the destination. It wasn't easy, or even possible, to buy just one ticket for your entire journey. This was because different railway lines were owned by different companies, and passengers had to pay each company separately at each stage of their journey.

What's on your ticket?

Have you ever thought about what's on your train ticket? Do you know what all the information means? Even those tiny numbers you've never noticed before? They all mean something and without them the whole ticketing system would fall into chaos.

Next time you travel on the railways, take a moment to look at your ticket. Each one is different, but how much of the following information can you identify?

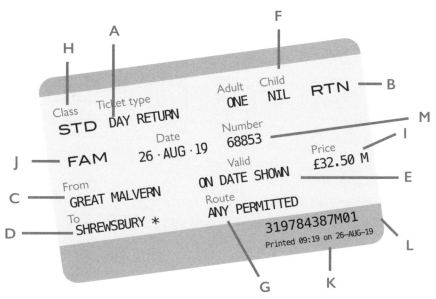

A: Ticket type: is it a single, return, or other type of ticket.

B: Direction of travel: for a return journey you'll get two tickets, one for your outward journey, and one for your inbound journey coming back.

C: Starting station: where your journey starts.

D: Destination station: where your journey finishes.

E: Date or dates you can travel: you might be allowed to travel for just one day, or over a week, or even a month.

F: Adult or child: is your ticket for an adult or child?

G: Information about any restrictions: routes you can't take or Train Operating Companies you can't travel with.

H: Ticket class: can you sit in first class on the train or standard class?

I: The price: how much you paid.

J: Railcard details: if you used a special discount card to buy your ticket it will be shown.

There's also details about how you paid for and printed your ticket:

K: Date and time: this is the date and time your ticket was printed.

L: Issuing point: a series of numbers that identifies which ticket office or machine the ticket was printed from.

M: Ticket number: every ticket has a unique number so that it can be traced in the railways' computer system as proof that this ticket was sold, and how much money was exchanged for it.

The First Ticket Office

The remains of one of the very first passenger ticket offices can be seen at Heighington station in County Durham. It's just a window in the side of the original station building, which would have been both a station house and a pub. The ticket window is now bricked up but still visible if you stop here to explore.

Also look out for the original station platform just in front of the ticket window and station building. Unlike platforms today, it's very close to the tracks and very low to the ground! You many not believe it, but trust us, this is where passengers once waited for the steam trains to come rolling in!

How did tickets change?

As the railways became more popular and more railways were built, companies began sharing their tracks. This created new routes and allowed more passengers to travel. There was of course a fee involved, which was calculated by how many passengers travelled on each particular route. But with each company writing tickets by hand, how could anyone really know how much money they were owed?

In 1836 Thomas Edmondson, a stationmaster at Milton station on the Newcastle and Carlisle Railway (now Brampton station), came up with the idea of producing pre-made tickets. They could be printed to include details of the starting and destination stations, total fare price, and class of ticket. Each ticket was also numbered so it would be easy to know exactly how many had been sold.

Edmondson's tickets were so revolutionary that some railway lines used them until the 1980s – that's more than 140 years in service. Even though technology now allows us to purchase and print tickets in lots of different ways, the basic and most important information included on our tickets today is exactly the same as the ones Edmondson introduced all those years ago.

18

Look out for!

Introduced in the 1980s at stations with limited or no ticket office facilities, the Permit to Travel machine (PERTIS) allowed passengers to pay a small amount of money (between five pence and one pound) for a permit to start their journey. This permit was then exchanged for a full-price ticket as soon as possible.

It is thought there are about 135 PERTIS machines left, and some of them still work! We've seen them at Haydons Road (South West London), Winsford (Cheshire), and Fishbourne (West Sussex) stations. Look out for them on your travels or visit the website: PERT.IS to search for the nearest machine to you (get your five-pence coins at the ready). How many can you find?

CHAPTER 6

BRIDGES, TUNNELS AND VIADUCTS

There are 30,000 bridges, tunnels, and viaducts on Britain's railways. Don't worry, we're not asking you to visit all of them. Just take a look at our top ten must-see list. How many do you think you can travel over, under, or through?

Travel Over an Amazing Bridge

19

Skerne Railway Bridge, Darlington

Part of the original Stockton and Darlington Railway, Skerne Bridge is the oldest railway bridge in the world that is still in use. The train crosses the bridge after Darlington and just before North End station. A pedestrian and cycle path now runs under the bridge, if you want to take a closer look. Access to the path is off John Street; just follow the river. When you get to the bridge, look out for the Transport Trust's red wheel plaque that marks the bridge's importance in British railway history.

- -

Barmouth Bridge, Gwynedd

The view as you cross the River Mawddach via Barmouth Bridge is one of the most impressive in the country and is not to be missed. Unusually, the bridge is mostly made from wood, which means it is constantly under attack by the sea and the creatures that live in it. This has led to a lot of repairs over the years. It is approximately 700 metres long and can be crossed on foot and by bike, as well as by the railway. As a pedestrian you are asked to contribute to an honesty toll that goes towards much-needed bridge maintenance.

Forth Bridge, Fife

The Forth Bridge carries two railway tracks across the Firth of Forth between North Queensferry and Dalmeny stations. The bridge is 2,467 metres long and weighs over 50,000 tonnes. It took 4,600 men and seven years to build, but despite its modern appearance it is in fact 130 years old. In 2015, the bridge was given UNESCO World Heritage status, which means it is recognised around the world as a masterpiece of its kind. As many as 200 trains cross the bridge every day – that's around 3 million passengers every year.

Tay Rail Bridge, Dundee

At 3,286 metres long the Tay is the longest rail bridge in Britain. It crosses the River Tay between Leuchars and Dundee stations. The bridge that now stands is the second to have been built. The first came to a very disastrous end in 1879 when it collapsed during a storm and killed over seventy people. The new bridge was made using over 25,000 tonnes of metal, 70,000 tonnes of concrete, and 10 million bricks.

Go Through a Tremendous Tunnel

Box Tunnel, Wiltshire

Perhaps the most famous railway tunnel in Britain was designed by Isambard Kingdom Brunel as part of the Great Western Railway's line from London to Bristol. The tunnel is 1.8 miles long and is located between Chippenham and Bath Spa stations. It took 4,000 men and five years to build. Construction started at both ends at the same time. When everyone eventually met in the middle, they discovered the two halves of the tunnel were only a few centimetres out of alignment. An incredible achievement considering Brunel, his team, and the men at work were digging by hand with only candles to light their way.

- -

Totley Tunnel, Derbyshire

Totley Tunnel is part of the Hope Valley Line that links the cities of Sheffield and Manchester. If you're starting your journey at Sheffield, the tunnel begins just past Dore and Totley station, and ends approximately 3.5 miles later just before Grindleford station. It is the second longest railway tunnel in Britain. It runs underneath the Peak District National Park (the first national park in Britain), so if you get off the train at Grindleford there is lots of exploring and beautiful walks you can try!

Go Over a Brilliant Viaduct

Harringworth Viaduct, Northamptonshire & Rutland

Confusingly known as the Harringworth viaduct, Welland viaduct and the Seaton viaduct, this is the longest brick viaduct in Britain, measuring just over 0.7 miles long. It is made of eighty-two arches; the first fifty-nine arches are in Northamptonshire, while arches sixty to eighty-two are in the county of Rutland. There are four East Midlands trains between Corby and Melton Mowbray stations (two in each direction) that cross the viaduct every weekday, but none at weekends.

- -

Cynghordy Viaduct, Carmarthenshire

Located along the Heart of Wales Line between Cynghordy and Sugar Loaf stations. The viaduct crosses the Bran Valley over the Afon Brân. It is 259 metres long, with eighteen arches built on a curve. It is one of only two viaducts on the entire line; the other is between Knucklas and Knighton stations, right by the border of Wales and England.

Knaresborough Viaduct, North Yorkshire

The viaduct at Knaresborough is so close to the station that the track points (the bits of track that move to guide trains onto different sections of the rails) are actually on top of it. This means some trains have to reverse onto the viaduct to travel back for their return journeys. It crosses the River Nidd at a staggering height of thirty metres. It is approximately 100 metres long with just four arches. While travelling over the viaduct gives you an incredible view of the town, the best view of the viaduct is actually from Knaresborough Castle, just a short five-to-seven-minute walk from the station.

- -

Glenfinnan Viaduct, Inverness-shire

Glenfinnan became one of the most famous viaducts in Britain after it appeared in the Harry Potter film, *Harry Potter and The Chamber of Secrets*. In the film Harry and Ron are chasing the Hogwarts Express in a flying car as it crosses the viaduct over the River Finnan. The viaduct is 380 metres long with twenty-one arches and is the longest concrete viaduct in Scotland. It is located between Locheilside and Glenfinnan stations on the West Highland Line to Mallaig. If you have time to stop at Glenfinnan there is a lovely station museum, a restored signal box, and even a dining car if you're in time for a spot of lunch.

CHAPTER 7

NUMBERS (PART ONE)

Which stations welcome the greatest number of passengers? Which places do only a few people visit each year? By knowing how many passengers use each station, TOCs can make sure there are enough trains in the right places to transport people where they need to go.

The figures are added up by an organisation called The Office of Rail and Road. They keep an eye on all the tickets that have been sold, and do some rather complicated maths to make sure they get the figures as accurate as possible. Every year, they share all the information they have for everyone to see.

Most and Least Used Stations 22

The most used station
2017–2018

Take a train to London Waterloo and join the 94,355,000 other people who did the exact same thing to make it Britain's busiest station. Between 750 and 800 trains leave Waterloo every day.

The least used station
2017–2018

With just forty passengers the entire year, Britain's least used station was … drum roll … Redcar British Steel, North Yorkshire.

There are currently just four trains that stop at the station each day, and from 2020 it is thought that services might not stop at all.

The most interchanges at a station
2017–2018

Not all journeys can be completed without having to change trains. Clapham Junction is where 29,604,407 passengers changed trains but only 29,444,741 people began or ended their journey there! Around 2,000 trains stop at Clapham Junction's seventeen platforms every day.

Look out for!

If you have time, see if you can find the rainbow plaque located on platform ten.
Rainbow plaques highlight the experiences of people from the LGBTQ+ community and this one is the first to be displayed at a railway station in Britain. It is dedicated to the famous poet Oscar Wilde, who, while changing trains at the station in 1895, was shouted and spat at by other passengers just because he was gay. The purpose of the plaque is to remind passengers about what happened and highlight how similar acts of prejudice will never again be tolerated on Britain's railways.

Geoff's Statistics

You might not be surprised to know that the top five most used mainline railway stations are all connected to lines on the London Underground. Take a look at the details and maybe you could combine a trip on a mainline service with one on the Underground too?

Most used stations	Connected to lines on the Underground
London Waterloo *(94,355,000 passengers)*	Bakerloo, Jubilee, Northern Lines
London Victoria *(74,66,512 passengers)*	District, Circle, Victoria Lines
London Liverpool Street *(66,966,512 passengers)*	Central, Circle, Hammersmith & City, Metropolitan Lines
London Bridge *(48,453,496 passengers)*	Jubilee, Northern Lines
London Euston *(44,745,816 passengers)*	Northern, Victoria Lines

CHAPTER 8

CLOCKS

Next time you're at a station, stop for a minute and take a look at the clocks. Each time you take a trip on the railways it's likely you've walked past more than a dozen clocks and not even noticed. We're here to tell you they're worth more of your time than you think (see what we did there).

Railway Time

Before there were railways in Britain, knowing the time wasn't as easy as checking your watch or looking at your phone. Only people of high status would own a clock; everyone else used a sundial. But sundial time is different depending where the sundial is located. A sundial in London, for example, might say 12 noon, while at the exact same moment a sundial in Penzance (Cornwall) will say 11.39 a.m.

To begin with, railway companies scheduled their trains using local sundial time. This meant some passengers might gain or lose a few minutes depending which direction they were going in. As more railways were built, and more railway lines crossed over each other, things became more complicated. After a while, some railway companies decided it would be better to set their timetables to just one time zone. It was the Great Western Railway in 1840 who were the first to do it. They chose Greenwich Mean Time (GMT), which also became known as Railway Time.

See Incredible Clocks

Clocks became (and still are) one of the most important objects on the railways. By the 1960s there were approximately 57,000 clocks across Britain's railways. Today, the exact number of clocks is difficult to calculate, particularly as so many of the electronic display boards and departure screens also include a small clock.

Cardiff Central Station

The clock tower at Cardiff Central station is a well-known landmark of the city. The station building you see today was built between 1932 and 1934.

In 2019, an unexpected guest took up residence underneath the clock. Next time you're at Cardiff Central Station, look very closely and you might just see the very tiny Welsh dragon that now lives on the clock tower. It keeps watch over the station and all the passengers who travel there.

Edinburgh Waverley

When railway stations were first built some had their own hotels and some were even part of the station itself. Passengers could walk directly from their train to their hotel room without even stepping outside – fancy.

A hotel like this was built at Edinburgh Waverley station in 1902. Today it's called the Balmoral Hotel and its original clock tower still looms high over the station. If you take a close look at the clock, however, you'll notice something unusual. Go on, look a little harder. That's right: it's three minutes fast. In fact, ever since it was built 117 years ago it's never actually told the time correctly. The clock was set three minutes fast on purpose, in the hope that passengers would never be late for their trains. There is only one occasion each year that the clock is set to tell the right time, and that's on New Year's Eve.

- -

London St Pancras International

The clock that hangs at the southern end of St Pancras station is one of the largest in Britain. It has a diameter of 5.49 metres and is made from aluminium with Welsh slate and twenty-three carat gold leaf on the numbers. It is a replica of the station's original clock, which was accidentally smashed in the 1960s. Luckily, Mr Hoggard, a guard who worked on the railway, was allowed to buy all the broken pieces for just twenty-five pounds, after which he spent years rebuilding it on the side of his barn in Nottinghamshire.

Eventually, when St Pancras was being refurbished in the 2000s London clockmakers Dent and Smith of Derby visited Mr Hoggard and used his clock as inspiration to make a brand-new replica for the station.

CHAPTER 9

STAFF

You probably see lots of train drivers and station staff every time you catch a train. But what about the people behind the scenes? Next time you pass a member of railway staff at a station, think about what job it is they might be doing. It could be one of these.

Can You Spot These People?

Tamper Trains and their Drivers

If you live or stay near a railway line, look out for a big yellow train slowly driving up or down the tracks.

Train tracks sit on top of a bed of loose stones (called ballast). Over time the weight of hundreds of trains passing along the tracks pushes the stones down into the earth. Some sink or dip further than others and almost every night Tamper trains are driven around the country straightening out all the dips and kinks.

They do this by lifting the tracks and driving tools into the ground that vibrate and move the ballast to realign the surface (a bit like fluffing up your pillow!).

Pest Controllers

Pigeons can cause lots of problems for the railway: they produce a lot of mess; they often steal passengers' food; and they can even suspend train services.

The solution at some stations, like King's Cross in London, is to call in the help of a well-trained Harris hawk. The hawk is looked after by a human handler who visits the station on a regular basis and releases the bird into the main concourse to scare away the pigeons.

- -

Air Operations

Network Rail uses helicopters and drones to take film footage and photographs of all the tracks and trackside equipment around the country. The cameras they use have 4K resolution and thermal imaging, which helps find electrical faults that the human eye cannot see on its own.

Did you know?

It's estimated that 240,000 people work for the railways.

207,840 (86.6 per cent) identify as <u>men.</u>

32,160 (13 per cent) identify as <u>women.</u>

The top three jobs on the railways are:

1 Infrastructure: 162,720 people work with railway infrastructure. This includes any kind of physical equipment, building or machinery that helps to make the railways run, like stations, railway tracks, and signalling systems.

2 Train Services: 60,960 people help to run the trains. This includes train drivers, guards, and anyone making sure that services are running at the correct station at the correct times so that passengers can get to their destination.

3 Rolling Stock: 13,440 people work with the trains. Testing, building, and maintaining them all day, every day.

CHAPTER 10

PROMINENT PEOPLE

Over the years there have been many important people who have shaped and changed the course of Britain's railways (pun intended). Discover their stories and see the places that have gone down in history.

The First Female Train Driver

Unbelievably, it took 212 years after the first public passenger railway service for the first woman to officially qualify as a mainline train driver in Britain. Her name was Anne Winter. On 1 May 1983, she drove her first passenger train from London Waterloo to Kingston station.

At the same time as Winter became a driver, there were several other women also on their way to sitting in the driver's seat. Celine Rocchia drove her first passenger train from London Victoria to Brighton.

Karen Harrison took her test around the same time as Rocchia and was well known as a driver but also as a member of the ASLEF trade union where she campaigned to ensure better working conditions and rights for all staff, but particularly for women.

One of Britain's first black female train drivers was Trudy Aarons. Aarons started her career as a train guard and qualified as a driver in the early 1990s. She drove trains around south London from Waterloo station and didn't retire until 2018 after an incredible twenty-nine years on the railways.

Take a Trailblazing Route

These pioneers were the first in Britain to prove how successful women train drivers can be. To celebrate their achievements, why not follow in their footsteps (or should we say 'train tracks') and make a journey along some of the routes they would have driven? Here are four to choose from.

● Anne Winter's Route:
London Waterloo to Kingston

All run by South Western Railway, there are LOADS of trains that will take you to Kingston from Waterloo station. Some are faster than others, some stop, and some are direct. There are just too many to list; you could literally turn up at the station and there would be a train ready to go within ten to fifteen minutes.

- -

● Celine Rocchia's Route:
London Victoria to Brighton

Both Southern Railways and the Gatwick Express service run regular trains to Brighton from Victoria station. Both options take about an hour (two hours return) but Southern will be cheaper (just saying).

Karen Harrison's Route:
London Marylebone to Banbury

Harrison worked at Marylebone station with Rocchia, driving trains along what is now the Chiltern Railways network. There are currently about three trains an hour between Marylebone and Banbury and the journey can take between fifty to eighty minutes.

- -

Trudy Aaron's Route:
London Waterloo to Hampton Court

Back at London Waterloo, South Western Railway runs two direct trains to Hampton Court station every hour. Of course, while you're at Hampton Court it would be rude not to take a visit to Hampton Court Palace, which is just across the road, and they even have a maze!

Geoff Fact!

The first female London Underground driver was Hannah Dadds, who qualified in 1978 (over four years before Anne Winter). There is a large plaque commemorating Dadds at Upton Park station on the District Line, which is where Hannah first worked when she joined the Underground as a 'railwaywoman'.

Fighting for Your Rights

In the 1960s, just sixty years ago, there was no law in Britain that stopped businesses, including the railway, from refusing to employ somebody because of the colour of their skin. A person's race could also be used as a reason to stop them getting a promotion, even if they were the most qualified for the job. At the time it wasn't illegal, but it wasn't right, and one man decided to do something about it.

Visit Asquith Xavier's Plaque

Dedicated to the man whose struggle to become Euston station's first black guard changed railway history. Find the plaque on the concourse at London Euston.

Asquith's story

Asquith Xavier moved from the Caribbean Island of Dominica to London in the 1950s. His first job on the railways was at Marylebone, where he worked as a porter and later became a guard.

In March 1966 Xavier applied to be a guard at Euston station, where staff were paid ten pounds more than those at Marylebone. Unfortunately, his application was quickly rejected, not because he didn't have the right experience, but because he was black and Euston, unlike Marylebone station, did not allow people of colour to work in jobs that had direct contact with passengers.

This kind of discrimination was sadly not unusual, and it was probably not the first time Xavier had been treated this way because of the colour of his skin. However, this time he decided he would not ignore it. He began writing letters to lots of important organisations, including the National Union of Railwaymen (a group set up to support railway workers).

Soon the newspapers started writing about what had happened and parliament also started asking questions. Then on 15 July 1966, the railways made an official announcement: people of colour would no longer be rejected from any roles at Euston station. Xavier was offered the job as a guard and he started a month later, in August 1966.

His bravery and his actions were an important moment for all people of colour working on the railways. After Euston, other stations began allowing anyone, no matter their race, to take on roles that they had previously been told they couldn't. Just two years later the Race Relations Act made it illegal for anyone in Britain to be denied the opportunity to work or be promoted because of the colour of their skin.

Navigating the Railways

There are roughly 20,000 miles of railway in Britain. The route taken by each line was carefully planned and designed by engineers, who often get the credit for the hard work that went into building it. But the railways were not built by a single person. That would be impossible! Instead, thousands of hardworking men risked their lives to make a path for the railways. They were known as 'navigators', or 'navvies', and without them the railways would not exist. Sadly, we don't even know their names.

Can You Cut It?

27

Every single mile of railway is a reminder of the work done by the navvies. But there are some places where you can see just how daring these men actually were.

Take a train from Liverpool Lime Street to Wavertree Technology Park and Broad Green stations. As you do, look out the window and notice the looming jagged sandstone slopes of what is known as the Olive Mount Cutting. It is called a 'cutting' because the navvies actually had to cut out a section of the earth to make way for the railway. The cutting is twenty-four metres deep and the navvies who built it used more than just pickaxes and shovels. They needed several blasts of gunpowder just to get started!

Navvy Work

To be a navvy you needed to be strong and fearless: you could have been digging a trench with a shovel through a field; building a bank on marshy ground; using gunpowder to blast open a cutting; or being lowered 180 metres underground to carve out a tunnel surrounded by water, with only a candle for light and a compass to guide you in the right direction.

Despite the dangers, there were no rules about safety and no hard-hats or protective clothing. Hundreds of men died in accidents or from injuries, but this didn't stop the work. Because while some railway companies and engineers treated navvies with respect, others saw them as nothing more than human machines. People could be replaced; the most important thing was to keep going and finish the railway as quickly as possible.

A Navvy Memorial ⟜ 28

There are only a few locations that honour the lives of the navvies and their families. People who risked everything to create the railways we know and use today. One of the most powerful memorials is in the small hamlet of Chapel-Le-Dale, just a couple of miles from the site of the Ribblehead Viaduct on the Settle and Carlisle Railway. Look inside the chapel and in the graveyard of St Leonards, you will find plaques dedicated to the memory of the men, women, and children who lost their lives while the railway was being built.

The best way to get there is via Ribblehead station, where there is a small exhibition that explains the history of the line, including information about the navvies who built it. You can then pop across the road to take a closer look at the staggering Ribblehead Viaduct.

Brunel's Masterpieces

Isambard Kingdom Brunel is often considered the greatest civil engineer to ever have worked on Britain's railways. Take a look at some of his best, and least, known works to decide how good he really was.

What made Isambard so great?

Brunel was certainly incredibly innovative and creative, often finding solutions to problems that no one had ever considered before. After studying at university, he trained as an apprentice with a horologist (the proper name for a clockmaker). His ability to understand how the smallest, most delicate mechanical movements (like the cogs inside a clock) have a huge effect on an entire machine gave him the vision to design and build some of his most revolutionary ideas.

Windmill Bridge, Hanwell

Catch a train and make the twenty-five-minute walk from either Southall or Hanwell stations until you reach the spot where Windmill Lane passes over the Grand Junction Canal, which passes over the railway. That's three modes of transport all crossing over each other at the same time. No matter how many times we see it, and read about it, we still can't work out how Brunel managed to build it without the canal flooding everywhere!

Thames Tunnel, Wapping

If you take a trip on the London Overground between Wapping and Rotherhithe stations, you'll be travelling through the world's first tunnel built under a navigable river. Press your face up against the train window (maybe give it a wipe first). The brick archways you see in the darkness are the original Thames Tunnel.

- -

Bristol Temple Meads

The station that greets you as you step off the train at Bristol Temple Meads is not the station designed by Brunel. To see that you have to walk just thirty seconds down the road to the corner of Station Approach and Temple Gate.

A lot has changed since Brunel's time. The building is now home to offices and spaces you can hire for events, but what you can still spot on the left-hand side is the gateway where arriving passengers once entered the station. The gateway for departing passengers – that would have been on the opposite, right-hand side – has long since gone.

While the original station is no longer in use, Brunel is still celebrated here as the man who brought the first passenger railway to Bristol. As you get ready to travel back, look out for the mosaic portrait of Brunel in the subway underneath the current platforms.

CHAPTER 11

NUMBERS (PART TWO)

Railway Measurements

Time to put your numbers hat back on, but this time we're talking distances. Take a trip to the highest, lowest, shortest, and longest stations.

Chains

Distances on the railways are measured using miles (just like roads) and chains. That's right, chains.

The method of using chains was invented by Edmund Gunter in the 1600s. He needed a way to measure plots of land accurately, even when they were not perfectly straight. To do this he used a length of chain, made up of equal-sized links. In Gunter's system there were 100 links per chain. The flexibility of the chain meant it could measure curves as well as straight lines – perfect for the railways (you might have noticed they don't always go in a straight line).

Travel Up and Down the Stations!

Highest Station

If you travel on the West Highland Line between Glasgow and Mallaig, you can stop at Corrour, officially the highest station in Britain at 408 metres above sea level.. As well as being the highest, Corrour is also one of the most isolated stations in the country. The only way to get there is by train or by walking the seventeen miles from the nearest public road.

- -

Lowest Station

Ryde Pier Head station on the Isle of Wight is the lowest station in Britain, at just one metre above sea level. Ryde Pier Head station is actually just off the coast of the Isle of Wight as the station is on a pier that stretches out into the Solent – the name given to the stretch of water between Portsmouth and the Isle of Wight.

Platforms

Longest Station Platform

The longest platform can be found at Gloucester station. It is 602.68 metres long (or 29.96 chains) and took Vicki six minutes to walk from one end to the other!

- -

Shortest Station Platform

The tiniest platform in Britain lives at Beauly station in Scotland. It's just 15.6 metres long. That's not even one chain!

Geoff Fact!

The best thing about getting a train from Ryde Pier Head station (apart from the fact that it travels along the pier) is that the trains themselves are old 1938 London Underground Tube trains. There are just eight stations on the Isle of Wight and it takes about twenty-five minutes to travel from one end of the line to the other.

Shortest Distance Between Stations

Go to the Welsh Valleys and ride on a train between Ty Glas and Birchgrove stations. The journey is just seventeen chains long, which is just under 342 metres (not even one lap around an athletics track). According to the Transport for Wales timetable, it takes just one minute to complete the journey. We think it could be less. Why not time it for yourself?

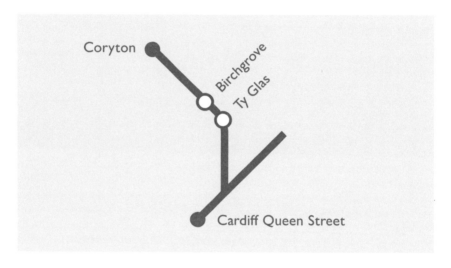

Look out for the zero point!

'Distance markers' are placed every quarter of a mile along the railway track so that staff can give accurate information about the location of any problems. The point at which a distance marker begins is different on different lines, and in different parts of the country. But no matter where they are, the starting location is always known as 'zero' point.

Longest Distance Between Stations

The award for the longest distance between two stations goes to Lockerbie and Kirknewton, Scotland, which are sixty-four miles and forty-two chains apart. Frustratingly, there is no train that stops at both stations. However, if you catch a service going from Carlisle to Edinburgh, the train will stop at Lockerbie and then travel through Kirknewton station. You just can't get off there.

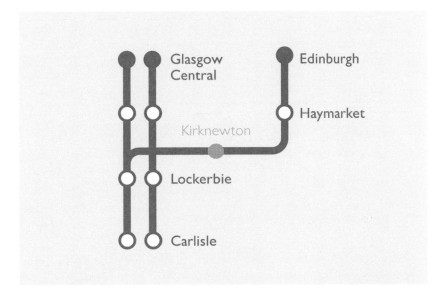

The most famous zero point in Britain is at York station. If you visit the station you can see a replica of the original marker, alongside a blue heritage plaque that explains that the station was once the zero point for ten different railway lines – many of which no longer exist.

CHAPTER 12

VICKI EXPLORES

The railways can connect you to all kinds of buildings, landscapes, people, and histories. Every place has its own story to tell and can help you better understand the communities around you. Discover a part of the country you've not been to before and learn why it was important enough to have a railway.

Castles by the Railways

Where you find a railway station, you'll often find a castle. This is because castles were always built in important locations: alongside a river where ships entered the country to bring vital food and goods; along a route that led to another more important city; or near the border between lands to protect the country from attack.

People were drawn to the safety that castles provided. Over time towns, villages, and cities were created. These were places that would later get their own railway stations.

Conwy Castle, Wales

Here the railway runs right next to Conwy Castle, crossing the River Conwy on a bridge that was designed to look like part of the castle walls, including a tower and battlements at one end.

Just before the train pulls into Conwy station, you will pass through the town walls and part of the castle's defences. When the railway was built in 1847, part of the town's original 560-year-old wall was knocked down and rebuilt with an archway that was wide enough to allow trains to travel through. The entrance to the castle is just a three-minute walk from the station.

The castle is located right on the edge of the River Conwy and is surrounded on almost three sides by water – the perfect defensive position, and best location to see your enemies approaching. If you visit the castle and climb to the top of one of the south-or east-facing towers you will get an incredible view across the river, including the approaching railway. Climbing any of the towers on the north or west side of the castle will give you a view over the town. The town walls can also be climbed and are one of the best ways to tour the town itself.

Newark Castle, Nottinghamshire

The station is called Newark Castle and the castle is also called Newark Castle. Just don't get confused between the two or you could be waiting a long time for a train!

The castle was built over 700 years before the railway arrived. It stands on the banks of the River Trent, now just a five-minute walk from the station. Both are protected by Historic England (an organisation that looks after the country's most important historical buildings).

The style of Newark Castle station was inspired by Italian architecture, dating back hundreds of years. It was one of the very first stations to be opened by the Midland Railway Company in 1846. Today, trains stop at the station on their way to and from Lincoln Central, Nottingham, Matlock, and Leicester.

Look out for!

Newark Castle played a large role during the First English Civil War (1642-1646). To find out more, you can follow the National Civil War Trail (a free app on your smart phone). It will lead you from the castle into the town of Newark itself.

Take a Train to Humber Bridge

34

Not many railways take you close to a bridge, but don't actually take you across it. However, this is exactly what happens at Barton-on-Humber station in North Lincolnshire.

The station is about a ten-minute walk from the Humber Bridge, which crosses the River Humber and connects North Lincolnshire to East Yorkshire. Today, if you want to travel from Barton-on-Humber to Hessle station (the first station on the other side of the bridge) by rail, you need to travel via Doncaster, which takes about three hours. Why not walk the three miles instead?

The Humber Bridge is a suspension bridge; this means the path of the bridge (where cars drive or people walk across) is held up by cables that hang down (suspended) from above. The bridge took seven years to build and measures 2,200 metres long.

Top tip!

The bridge is open every day of the year, but you should always check the weather as high winds can make crossing the bridge dangerous. Also, remember that cars can travel up to 50 mph on the bridge, so always take care when walking.

The Hardy Tree

Sometimes it's not the biggest, longest, or tallest sites that tell the greatest stories. To discover one such example, take a short five-minute walk from London St Pancras station, down Midland and St Pancras Road, to St Pancras Old Church.

Here in the graveyard you'll find an ash tree. The base of the tree is encircled by headstones; not surprising in a graveyard you might think, but these headstones are different. They are packed so tightly around the tree they look as though they have grown from its roots.

It is known as the Hardy Tree, named after Thomas Hardy, who was a famous British writer from the nineteenth and twentieth century. It was Hardy himself who placed the headstones around the tree, not for any artistic purposes but because it was his job. In the 1860s, before he was a writer, Hardy worked for an architecture company. His job was to clear away parts of the graveyard (bodies as well as headstones) to make way for the new St Pancras station.

Not far from the tree, you'll find a large brick wall at the back of the graveyard. Behind that wall are the busy railway lines taking trains in and out of St Pancras station.

The Hardy Tree reminds us that in Victorian times nothing could stand in the way of the railways, not even the dead.

Churches and Cathedrals

One of the easiest landmarks to spot while travelling on the railways are churches and cathedrals (with their enormous spires they don't really blend into the background). There are a few, however, that particularly stand out and are well worth getting off the train to take a closer look at.

The Crooked Spire

No matter from what direction you arrive at Chesterfield station, you cannot fail to see the nearby parish church spire from the train window. The first thing you might notice is how crooked it is. Not even just a little bit crooked, but very crooked. So crooked that as you stare up at it, you'll wonder how on earth it manages to stay up – especially on a windy day.

The story of Chesterfield's spire starts in 1361 when it was first added to the church's tower. It was built using wood and measured 69.49 metres tall. About 300 years later a decision was made to cover the spire in lead tiling to help protect the wood from the damaging effects of the weather. It was then that things started to take a different shape.

The lead tiling is extremely heavy, much heavier than the wood underneath. It is also affected by the temperature, getting ever so slightly bigger when it is hot, then shrinking ever so slightly when it cools down. Some people think that the combination of the weight and its constant changing size has forced the wood underneath to twist with the pressure.

Seems to make sense, right? Well, this is just the theory. No one really knows for certain as nothing like this has ever happened to another church. What we do know is that the spire is leaning 2.9 metres away from where it should be, and there's no stopping it – it's still moving to this day!

Look out for!

There are tours of the spire led by staff and volunteers at the church. You will climb up inside the tower and see how twisted it actually is. It looks even more twisted on the inside than it does on the outside – if that's even possible!

A World Heritage Site

Durham Cathedral is part of a UNESCO (United Nations Education, Scientific and Cultural Organisation) World Heritage Site that includes Durham Castle (right next door to the cathedral). This means it is recognised as a place of historical and cultural importance. There are currently only 1,121 places in the entire world that have been given UNESCO status, which makes Durham extremely special.

When you look at Durham Cathedral from Durham station, the size and scale of the building makes it feel much closer than it actually is – and that's because it's huge! It still only takes about fifteen minutes to walk there so there's no excuse not to visit.

It was built nearly 1,100 years ago between 1093 and 1133, and it still has lots of its original features, like its stone vaulted ceiling, one of the first to be built using new techniques with stone rather than wood. This changed the way cathedrals were built for the next 400 years. (Durham Cathedral was a bit of a trendsetter).

The cathedral also has three original copies of the Magna Carta. Written in 1215, it was the first legal document that officially said Kings and Queens needed to follow the law just like everyone else. It also established the idea that all people were entitled to justice and a fair trial. While the exact rules have changed a lot over the years, the ideas first written in the Magna Carta are still the foundation of Britain's laws and system of governance today.

Going into Battle

The platform signs at Battle station in East Sussex always make us feel like we're travelling back in time. 'Alight here,' they say, 'for 1066'. If time travel was possible, Battle in October 1066 would have been one of the most dangerous places to visit. For it was here that the armies of Harold, King of England, and William, Duke of Normandy in France, engaged in one of the deadliest fights on British soil.

Thankfully, Battle is now a peaceful and beautiful town. A fifteen-minute walk from the station will take you to Battle Abbey, where the battle, now known as the Battle of Hastings (the town of Hastings is about 6.4 miles away), is thought to have taken place.

But what were Harold and William fighting about? Well, despite the fact that Harold had officially been made King of England earlier that year, William believed the title belonged to him and he wanted to take it back.

Spoiler alert – Harold was killed and Battle Abbey was later built under the orders of the new King William I (also known as William the Conqueror, for obvious reasons). It is said that the high altar in the abbey was built on the exact spot where Harold died.

Crossing the Border

Take an adventure via the East Coast Mainline and stop at Berwick-upon-Tweed to discover the history of an English (and Scottish) border town. Carry on into Scotland and see if you can spot the crossing sign – you'll have to be quick; the train doesn't slow down!

Where does Berwick belong?

For hundreds of years, the Scottish and the English fought over land and who would be its King or Queen. While people in both countries were affected by the fighting, there was perhaps one town that suffered more than any other: Berwick-upon-Tweed.

If you take a look at a map today, you'll see that Berwick-upon-Tweed is located in the very north of England, just three miles from the Scottish border. It is the very last English town where the train stops before crossing the border and heading to Edinburgh.

However, for 300 years Berwick was an important port for Scotland. That is, until the end of the thirteenth century when Edward I captured the town and declared it part of England. Over the next 200 years, Berwick was passed back and forth between the two countries, and back and forth again, and again, until 1482 when it was captured for the very last time. It has officially been part of England ever since.

Yet despite what the map says, the town still has strong connections to Scotland. The local football club, Berwick Rangers, plays in the Scottish football leagues, and secondary school students can choose to study in Scotland rather than in the English schools in Berwick.

Take some time to explore the town – and in particular the town walls – the castle ruins, Berwick Barracks, and any of the local museums to learn more about what life was like living in a border town.

Look out for!

One of the most picturesque views of Berwick is from the railway itself, which crosses the River Tweed via the Royal Borders Bridge. Made of twenty-eight arches, the bridge is thirty-eight metres at its tallest part and measures 656 metres from one end to the other. The railway bends before and after arriving at Berwick so you get an incredible view of the bridge no matter what direction you're travelling in.

Spotting the Boundary Sign

As you cross the border between England and Scotland see if you can spot the sign marking the exact location. As the train travels so quickly you might not be able to spot it without some help. We suggest filming through the window (if you're heading north make sure you're looking out the right-hand side) and play it back slowly until you spot the sign.

CHAPTER 13

STATION NAMES

Your Favourite Station

What is your favourite railway station name?
How do stations even get their names?
Some seem obvious, like Norwich station, which is
(you've guessed it) in Norwich, but other stations
have much more interesting stories to tell. Here's a
few of our favourites to get you started.

Bat & Ball, Kent

This station was named after a pub, the Bat & Ball Inn, which sadly
no longer exists. When the station opened it was originally just called
Sevenoaks, but then another station opened nearby that was also
called Sevenoaks – what are the chances?! To prevent any confusion,
the name was changed to Sevenoaks Bat & Ball, but eventually it just
became known as Bat & Ball. If you stop for a visit, make sure you
look inside the station house, which has recently been restored and is
open to the public. It hosts events throughout the year and is home
to a delicious cafe selling local produce. Yum.

Shippea Hill, Cambridgeshire

When it opened in 1845, Shippea Hill was called Mildenhall Road. Forty years later it was renamed Burnt Fen, and then nineteen years after that it was given its current name, Shippea Hill. Ironically the 'hill' it's named after is less than five metres high, but the land in this part of the country is extremely flat, so that's quite a steep gradient!

- -

Longest Station Name

Some of you might be thinking you know the answer to this one. The longest station name in Britain is that really long Welsh one, Llanfairpwllgwyngyllgogerychwyrndrobwllllantysiliogogogoch. While you would be right, you are also wrong. Sorry. According to the national rail database, the station's official name is just Llanfairpwll. So, this makes the longest station name in Britain (drum roll, please) Rhoose Cardiff International Airport. (We know, it's a bit disappointing isn't it.)

According to the history books, the long version of Llanfairpwll is believed to have been created during the nineteenth century. It was invented as a way to encourage people to stop and visit the local area. It certainly worked. More than 20,000 visitors now stop at the station every year just to see the incredibly long station signs that feature the full version, proudly displayed on both of the platforms and the station building.

Sign Language

41

The other great thing about station names in Britain is that not all of them are in English. There are four places in the country where this happens; can you visit some of them?

Abertawe

Swansea

Wales: as you travel round Wales you'll see that all station signs are written in both Welsh and English. Welsh is always first.

Aberdeen

Obar Dheathain

Scotland: throughout Scotland, station signs are written in both English and Scottish Gaelic. English is always first.

Southall

ਸਾਉਥਹਾਲ

Southall station, West London: the platform signs are in both English and Punjabi. This celebrates the large Punjabi population who live in the community.

Way Out

进出口

Bicester Village, Oxfordshire: As Bicester welcomes thousands of Chinese visitors every year; the signs and announcements at the station are in both English and Mandarin.

CHAPTER 14

NATURE AND THE RAILWAYS

Wherever there is a railway there is wildlife. What might look like abandoned land running alongside the tracks is in fact home to thousands of different species of insects, animals, plants, and flowers. You might be surprised at just how much the railway, rather than being destructive, can help nature thrive.

Tree Spotting

How many different species of tree do you think you can identify? There are certainly plenty to choose from. It is thought there are around 10 million trees growing next to and close by the railways in Britain.

Next time you're out and about keep your eyes peeled for some of the biggest and most common railway trees:

Ash . . . . ☐

Horse chestnut . . . . ☐

Lime . . . . ☐

Poplar . . . . ☐

Sweet chestnut . . . . ☐

Sycamore . . . . ☐

Leaves on the Line

With trees come leaves, and leaves mean delayed trains. For a long time, we couldn't work out how a few little leaves could stand in the way of a huge metal train, but then we discovered that a large tree sheds between 10,000 and 50,000 leaves every year (that's a lot of leaves). What happens to those leaves then causes the problems …

When a train runs over the leaves, it squishes them and all the juice from inside forms a slippery layer that makes it difficult for trains to stop. This forces the driver to go slowly. To get rid of this slippery surface the railway has sixty-one 'leaf-busting' trains that travel all around the country cleaning the lines using high-pressure water jets. As well as blasting away leaves, these trains also cover the rails in a mixture of sand and metal fragments to help trains grip the track better. Leaf-busting trains can be used at any time of the day, so it's likely you'll see them on your travels, especially during the autumn. (There is also a team of people who remove the leaves by hand if needed – they are on standby twenty-four hours a day!)

Getting Close to Nature

Every time a new piece of engineering work takes place it could completely destroy the homes of wildlife living nearby. To stop this happening, Network Rail consults with Natural Resources Wales, Natural England, and Scottish Natural Heritage to identify animals and their habitats and find ways to protect them while they do their work.

The land alongside the railways can be seen from the train windows but getting access is dangerous. It is for staff only. Don't panic though, there are lots of amazing places where you can get up close to nature while also taking the train.

Berney Marshes, Norfolk

Take a train to Berney Arms station and when you get off you'll find yourself standing on a small, unsheltered platform in the middle of an RSPB nature reserve.

Follow one of the signed trails but be aware there are no facilities in the marshes or at the station; it's just you and nature, so make sure you're prepared. What there are lots of are birds. Thousands and thousands of wintering ducks, geese, and swans. The best times to see them are in autumn and winter.

Be especially careful about the train times coming back. The services are limited and the station is a request stop, which means you have to stick your arm out to signal that you would like the train to stop.

Arthog Bog, Mawddach Valley

Arthog Bog wetland reserve, just a few metres from Morfa Mawddach station, is full of incredible wildlife. It is another RSPB site and also listed as a Site of Special Scientific Interest. This means the land and plants that grow here are protected by law because of what they tell us about the area's natural history.

- -

New Cross Gate Cutting, London

Located between New Cross Gate and Brockley stations on the London Overground, the New Cross Gate cutting is an area of oak woodland with lots of wildlife and around 170 species of flowering plants.

The cutting was made for the railway between 1838 and 1939 and its steep banks have been reclaimed by nature over the years, creating a wonderful hidden gem right in the heart of suburban London. The cutting isn't open all the time, so make sure you check the London Wildlife Trust website before you make a visit.

- -

Lewes Railway Land Wildlife Trust

Created on the site of the old rail yards and sidings, the Lewes Railway Land Nature Reserve is now full of wildlife that is supported by the Winterbourne Stream and the River Ouse.

The entrance to the reserve is about a ten-minute walk from Lewes station, down Railway Lane, and through an old level-crossing gate. Paths and walkways are easy to follow, and everything is fully accessible for those looking for a step-free route.

Incredible Edible

Incredible Edible is an idea, an organisation, and a movement that inspires local communities to work together to plant and grow food that can be shared by everyone. Look out for edible gardens at stations around the country.

Be Inspired

More and more communities are starting to create edible planters and gardens at their local stations. It's a great way to learn about gardening, to make new friends, and to support people living in your area. Why not join your nearest group or even start your own? You could take some inspiration from any of the following stations where edibles are grown in abundance:

Winchester, Hampshire .... ☐

Machynlleth, Powys .... ☐

Rose Hill, Stockport .... ☐

West Kirby, Wirral .... ☐

You can visit the official website to find out more: https://www.incredibleedible.org.uk

Todmorden, West Yorkshire

The first Incredible Edible project started in the town of Todmorden. A group of locals decided to take over unused and unloved public spaces to grow fruit, vegetables, and herbs that anyone could pick and eat.

Their actions were so positive and so successful that the entire town is now packed full of edible spaces, including Todmorden railway station. The town holds regular events centred around growing and using local food. Even the local secondary school now teaches agriculture to support young people's interest in planting their own food.

To help visitors see all the different spaces involved in the project, there is a downloadable walking tour from the Incredible Edible Todmorden website. The first stop is the station. You'll find lots of planters on the platforms that grow herbs for commuters to pick on their way home.

- -

Severn Beach Line

Take a train along the Severn Beach Line from Bristol and you will notice that each station has its own 'cycle stand' planters (convenient for your bike and for garnishing your evening meal). On the first Friday of every month, groups of volunteers from the Bristol branch of Incredible Edible get together to look after the planters. Anyone can join in. All you have to do is sign up via the events page on their website.

Another project has just started at Avonmouth station. Look behind Platform 2 to see how the station's new community garden is progressing. The garden grows food that can be picked by local people and is also used for the lunch club at Avonmouth Community Centre near the station.

Non-Edible Gardens

Not all station gardens are edible (for humans, at least). There are lots of stations where non-edible plants, flowers, and trees are gardened to create a tranquil place for passengers and help bring back wildlife to the area.

Bingley, West Yorkshire

Part of the Leeds and Liverpool Canal is tucked between Bingley and Crossflatts stations. Here you'll find the Five Rise Lock, a series of five canal locks that follow on from each other to create a 'staircase lock'. It is the steepest staircase lock situated on the longest canal in Britain. It takes about fifteen minutes to walk to the lock from Bingley station. (Don't get confused with the three-rise lock that is also nearby.) If you don't have time to see the real thing, you can always enjoy a replica in the garden at the station.

The garden can be found on Platform 2. It was designed and created by 'Action Stations' (great name) and includes bird and bat boxes, plus an eight-metre-long flower planter in the shape of a canal boat.

If you do have time to walk along the canal there is lots of wildlife to spot, such as dragonflies, butterflies, ducks, and even otters! You can download a wildlife guide from the Canal & River Trust website.

Bottesford, Leicestershire

Travel along the brilliantly named Poacher Line from Nottingham
to Skegness and stop off at Bottesford station. Here you'll discover
an award-winning community garden known locally as the 'BFG'
(Bottesford Friendly Garden). It is home to bee-friendly wildflowers,
fruit trees, a pond, hedgehog ramps, and even a bug hotel. The garden
was created by volunteers from the local area and designed by students
from the local primary school in collaboration with the Poacher Line
Community Rail Partnership and The Bee-Friendly Trust.

An old station building is included in the garden, which will
eventually become an education centre for school groups and
railway visitors to learn about gardening and wildlife. The garden
won 'Most Enhanced Station Buildings and Surroundings' in the
2019 Community Rail Awards.

Look out for!

While you're at Bottesford, why not
take a walk along the 'Walks by Train'
route from Bottesford to Aslockton
(download a map and guide from the Lincolnshire County
Council website). The adventure is ten kilometres long and will
take you from Leicestershire to Nottinghamshire, through the
surrounding countryside, and past a disused railway line. You'll
even get a cracking view of Bottesford village, which includes
the spire of St Mary's church, one of the tallest in Leicestershire.

Westhoughton, Bolton

There isn't any another station in Britain that has bigger gardens than those in Westhoughton. They run the entire length of both platforms and are jam-packed with plants, flowers, bird boxes, gnomes, artworks, and classic enamel advertising signs. There is no station building here, only ticket machines and shelters on the platforms. The gardens are the station's main feature, and they really make a huge difference to the look of the place.

The gardens were created and are cared for by the Friends of Westhoughton Station. When we visited Westhoughton we were mostly intrigued by a large wooden cow that had been displayed just underneath one of the platform signs. It had a wooden saw hovering behind its head and the word 'Howfen' written underneath.

We discovered that the word 'Howfen' is used to abbreviate the name of the town. The cow is linked to a local legend about a farmer who discovered a cow had its head stuck in the farm gate. Rather than sawing the gate apart, the farmer sawed the cow's head off instead. (The cow didn't cost as much as the gate.) There's no evidence that this actually happened, but the story has been told so many times it's become well known among the locals.

Depending on what time of year you visit Westhoughton, you will see different things in bloom in the gardens. At Christmas there is usually an additional display of festive trees, and sometimes Santa even drops by on his sleigh. (We knew Santa preferred travelling by train!)

Largs, North Ayrshire

Largs is best known for being the site where the Vikings tried to invade Scotland in 1263. They did not succeed. But throughout this seaside town there are plenty of reminders. Even the new community garden at Largs station exhibits the bow (front end) of a Viking boat.

The station garden was created by volunteers and officially opened in 2018. You'll find it just behind Platform 2. It includes hundreds of flowers and plants, a giant chess board, and a path that was built from a disused public square, which makes it completely accessible for wheelchair users and those with buggies.

Railway Pets

As well as the wildlife that lives close to the railways, there are also animals who live at stations and can be just as important as any human member of staff. (They often have bigger Facebook groups and more Twitter followers!)

Some stations even have plaques dedicated to the memory of past pets. Next time you're at Fishguard and Goodwick station, for example, look out for the statue of the station's beloved railway cat, who was buried under the railway bridge in 1930.

Here is where you can find just a few of today's most notorious railway pets.

Felix and Bolt, the Huddersfield Station Cats

As you're waiting for a train at Huddersfield station, you might encounter two confident-looking cats patrolling the platforms. Meet Felix and Bolt, pest controllers for TransPennine Express.

Felix is Senior Pest Controller, having worked at the station since 2011, and is so well known she even has her own Facebook group (with over 135,000 followers). In 2017, a book about her adventures was published and instantly became a best-seller.

Bolt, Junior Pest Controller, arrived in 2018 and has quickly been learning all his duties from Felix. Truly a pest control team to be reckoned with!

Percy, Okehampton Station Cat

For the last three years the resident pest controller at Okehampton station in Devon has been Percy. His duties are so important that he has been given his own equipment, including a cat(flap) entrance to the signal box, and a personalised hi-vis jacket.

Percy joined the staff at Okehampton after being rescued by a local cattery. You can follow Percy on Facebook, or for a chance to see him in person you'll need to plan a trip to Okehampton quite carefully. Trains from Exeter only run on Sundays during the summer months (usually May–September).

At Okehampton, you can also ride the Dartmoor Railway, a heritage line that takes you all the way to the incredible Meldon Viaduct and back (after saying hello to Percy, of course).

Ruswarp, Station Dog

Ruswarp's owner was Graham Nuttall, the co-founder of the Friends of the Settle–Carlisle Line. In the 1980s Ruswarp was the only non-human to sign the petition to stop the line from closing. His paw print was included along with all the other human signatures.

In 1990 Ruswarp and Graham went walking in Wales. Along the way, Graham became unwell and sadly died. Ruswarp refused to leave his friend and stayed by Graham's side for eleven weeks until rescuers finally discovered them. A statue of Ruswarp was erected in his honour at Garsdale station, which was thought to be their favourite spot.

CHAPTER 15

SEEING THE FUTURE

Since the Oystermouth Railway opened
213 years ago, a lot has changed on
Britain's railways.

The next big changes we'll see as passengers are new
trains (meaning new moquettes!), the doubling of
tracks (meaning faster services!), and new stations
(meaning more places to explore!).

New Trains

Let's talk about trains first. There are already new trains on the railways, but over the next few years more modern trains will be used, and the old trains will gradually disappear. So, for now, see how many of the following new trains you can encounter, and if you're lucky enough to take a ride on one, snap a picture of the moquette.

Azuma

This is the name given to the new Intercity Trains used by LNER on the East Coast Mainline. If you're jumping on a train from London King's Cross to York or Edinburgh, you may be lucky enough to find yourself on one of these.

- -

Pacer Replacer

Okay that's not their 'official' name, but it's what we like to call them. They're actually called Class 195 (diesel) and Class 331 (electric) trains, and they will replace the much loved, and hated, Pacer trains that have been travelling around the country since the 1980s.

Nova 3

Technically the new bit of the Nova 3 trains (great name by the way) is the carriages, not the locomotive (engine). They belong to TransPennine Express and there are a total of 65 new carriages out on the network. You'll most likely see them as a set of five carriages being pulled by a Class 68 locomotive. They're currently used on the lines between Liverpool and Scarborough, and Manchester Airport and Middlesbrough.

FLIRT – Fast Light Intercity and Regional Trains

You can find these intriguingly named new trains all around the Greater Anglia network. While most people call them 'FLIRT', they do have a technical Class name, which is 745 and 755. The greatest thing about these Greater Anglia trains is that they are bi-mode. This means they are both electric and diesel and are not restricted to only one part of the railway network. Clever.

Geoff's Wild Card

For the last in our list of new trains I thought I'd sneak in a mention of the Glasgow Subway (a circular fifteen-station Metro system under the streets of Glasgow). We hear rumours that brand new trains will be arriving some time in 2020. That's all the information we have. Keep your ear to the (under) ground.

New Stations ⟢ 49

Fingers crossed there are already three new stations for you to visit. All of which opened at the end of 2019.

Worcestershire Parkway

This station connects two previously separate railway lines. The line between Oxford, Worcester, and Hereford, which is run by the Great Western Railway, and the line between Cardiff, Birmingham, and Nottingham, which is served by CrossCountry trains. Before the station was built, the two lines crossed but there was never any way for passengers to connect between the two without travelling miles out of the way.

The biggest challenge when building this station were the three new station platforms, which all measured 250 metres long. They each needed to be constructed in smaller sections, away from the tracks, and then slotted into place piece by piece.

The best way to tick off this station would be to arrive on one line, and then depart from the other.

Warrington West

Located (unsurprisingly) west of the town of Warrington, this brand new station can be found on the Cheshire Line between Liverpool and Manchester. The centre of Warrington already has two stations, but this one will support communities on the outskirts of the town.

With three train services every hour this will be an easy station to visit either on Northern or East Midlands trains.

Robroyston

This is Glasgow's sixtieth station (we often forget how huge Glasgow is) and can be found between Springburn and Stepps stations along the line from Glasgow Queen Street to Cumbernauld. It is built on the exact same location as the original Robroyston station that opened in 1898 and closed in 1956.

Next Stop...

Like us, you'll be pleased to know that the list of new stations doesn't stop there.

Over the next few years there are many more being built, but as yet there are no specific dates for each one. This means you have plenty of time to prepare your visit. Going to new stations on opening day, and arriving in time for the first train service, is a momentous and historical moment! A photo of yourself in front of the station sign is an absolute must. Keep your eyes and ears open for information about the following new projects:

Dalcross: situated near Inverness.

Reading Green Park: this will be on the line between Reading and Basingstoke.

Kintore: located on the line north of Aberdeen.

Crossrail's Elizabeth Line: yes, we know this is a line and not a station, but it will have five brand new stations that will open once the line is complete.

While so much has changed over the years, the one thing that remains the same is the importance of the railways to different communities around the country. Railways aren't just about getting people from A to B, they're also about connecting people to friends and family, and offering new opportunities for adventures that wouldn't otherwise be possible. For that reason, we hope they continue to grow and change. To the trains!

Bibliography

Bradley, Simon, **The Railways: Nation, Network & People**, Profile Books Ltd, 2015

Coleman, Terry, **The Railway Navvies: A History of the Men who Made the Railways**, Head of Zeus, 2015

Dobrzynski, Jan, **British Railway Tickets**, Shire Publications, 2011

Guy, Andy and Jim Rees, **Early Railways 1569 – 1830**, Shire Publications, 2016

Jenkins, Simon, **Britain's 100 Best Railway Stations**, Penguin Random House, 2017

Stewart, M.G, **British Platform Tickets to 1948**, The Transport Ticket Society, 1986

Jones, Robin, **Great British Railway Firsts: How Britain Led the World in Rail Technology**, Mortons Media Group Ltd, 2019

Laws, Bill, **Fifty Railways that Changed the Course of History**, David&Charles, 2016

Lyman, Ian, **Railway Clocks**, Mayfield Books, 2004

Marsden, Colin J, **2019-2020 Rolling Stock Review**, Key Publishing Ltd, 2019

Moore, Kate, **Felix the Railway Cat**, Penguin Random House, 2017

The Leeds – Settle & Carlisle Railway, The Settle Carlisle Railway Development Company, 2017

Wojtczak, Helena, **Railway Women: Exploitation, Betrayal and Triumph in the Workplace**, The Hastings Press, 2005

Wolmar, Christian, **A Short History of Trains**, DK, 2019

Websites

These websites can help you find out more information about the facts mentioned in this book, and provide ideas for your own adventures.

Association of Community Rail Partnerships - https://communityrail.org.uk

ASLEF - https://www.aslef.org.uk

Cadw - https://cadw.gov.wales

Canal River Trust - https://canalrivertrust.org.uk

Crooked Spire - https://crookedspire.org

Dent London - http://www.dentlondon.com

Devon and Cornwall Rail Partnership - https://dcrp.org.uk

Durham World Heritage Site - https://www.durhamworldheritagesite.com

English Heritage - https://www.english-heritage.org.uk

Forth Bridge - https://www.theforthbridges.org

Glasgow Central Tours - https://www.glasgowcentraltours.co.uk

Head of Steam Museum - https://www.head-of-steam.co.uk

Heart of Wales Line - https://www.heart-of-wales.co.uk

Historic England - https://historicengland.org.uk

Historic Environment Scotland - https://www.historicenvironment.scot

Humber Bridge - https://www.humberbridge.co.uk

I. K. Brunel - http://www.ikbrunel.org.uk

Incredible Edible - https://www.incredibleedible.org.uk

Transport Trust - https://www.transporttrust.com

Science and Industry Museum - https://www.scienceandindustrymuseum.org.uk

Network Rail - https://www.networkrail.co.uk

National Civil War Centre - http://www.nationalcivilwarcentre.com

National Railway Museum - https://www.railwaymuseum.org.uk

Railsigns - https://www.railsigns.uk

RSPB - https://www.rspb.org.uk

Smith of Derby - https://www.smithofderby.com

St Pancras Old Church - https://posp.co.uk/st-pancras-old-church/

UNESCO - https://whc.unesco.org

Visit 1066 - https://www.visit1066country.com

Wild London - https://www.wildlondon.org.uk

Thank You

This book would not have been possible without the help and support of so many people. We would like to say a huge thank you to the following;

Harriet Birkinshaw
Elizabeth Clayton
Martin Clitheroe
Mark Cooper
Phil Dickinson
Dave Green
Dave Kirwin
Simon Weller (ASLEF)
Sophia Moor (DfT)
Hannah MacDonald
Dave McCormick
Warren Pilkington
PERT.IS
Kai Michael Poppe
Sarah Wray

A special thanks to Emily Sear for the book design and Grace Helmer for the beautiful illustrations she has created, which really bring the book to the life.

Index
of Trains,
Stations
and Lines

Ride the tube like never before and discover the top 50 unusual things to do and see on the London Underground.

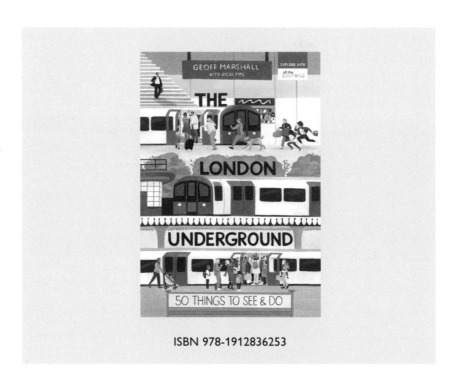

ISBN 978-1912836253

Bursting with facts and activities from YouTube train expert Geoff Marshall with additional sights to see from his co-creator of All the Stations, Vicki Pipe, this book will inspire children – and adults – to seize the moment and explore the hidden world of London's Underground.